Congratulations!

You've made the choice to learn the vocabulary most often tested on the SAT rather than memorize a bunch of definitions that will NOT be tested. Smart.

This SAT Vocabulary Builder Series is dedicated to drilling the **578** most essential--most heavily tested--SAT words. My students drill with these puzzles and the other puzzle books to put the vocabulary into practice rather than memorizing a bunch of dry definitions. The SAT Essentials Series covers these most essential SAT words in Word Games and Story Writing Drills and Math acuity through Number Games. Interested in less painful prep? Get **200** free games and access to the entire series. Use the QR code or visit:

https://www.prepwise.com/puzzles

How to Use

Each Puzzle is testing you on **10** words from the master SAT Essentials list. The Crossword Clues should give you context for how a word might actually be used in speech or writing. These are not definitions. These are contextual clues.

With over **30** years of experience helping students prepare for the SAT, I have found that those who focus on flash cards don't do nearly as well as my students who use the vocabulary games and story writing drills. The SAT is not testing you on your ability to regurgitate a definition. So ... stop that. You'll make FAR MORE progress by incorporating the target words into your everyday language.

These crossword games are written to help you focus on a manageable chunk of information in a single sitting. Each puzzle offers **10** clues that point to the target words on the SAT Essentials list. Each target vocabulary word has several different crossword clues so you may see the same tested word within a single book with totally different clues. This is done to sneak the word into your brain without forcing you to memorize anything. Memorization leads to poorer outcomes than using the target vocabulary. Since using many of these words in your actual everyday life is challanging ... or awkward, lean on these games to get your practice.

Across

2. Standing at polar ends

3. Determined quality

6. Endlessly desiring

8. Ideal exemplar

9. One on one conversation

10. Flow of goods from production to distribution

Down

1. Dealing with or directing

4. Feeling two ways at once

5. Cooperative association

7. Detail-oriented

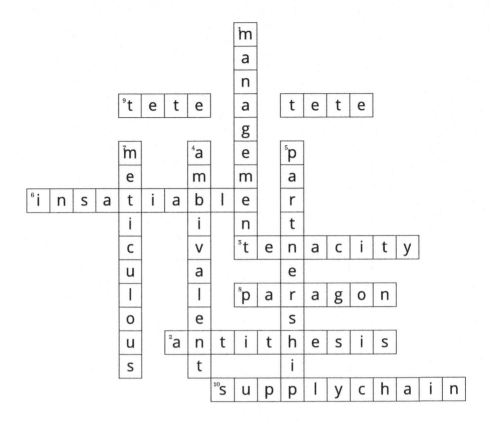

Across

2. Standing at polar ends
3. Determined quality
6. Endlessly desiring
8. Ideal exemplar
9. One on one conversation
10. Flow of goods from production to distribution

Down

1. Dealing with or directing
4. Feeling two ways at once
5. Cooperative association
7. Detail-oriented

Across

2. Erase from a surface

3. Long and supple

4. Harsh auditory mess

6. To praise highly

7. Culturally detached

Down

1. Overstating one's importance

5. Indulge in enjoyable festivities

8. Wrongdoings personified

9. Not lasting

10. Make a task easier

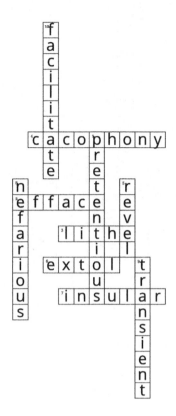

Across

2. Erase from a surface

3. Long and supple

4. Harsh auditory mess

6. To praise highly

7. Culturally detached

Down

1. Overstating one's importance

5. Indulge in enjoyable festivities

8. Wrongdoings personified

9. Not lasting

10. Make a task easier

Across

3. Land left to restore fertility

4. Income from business operations

5. Plentiful

6. Privilege granted as an honor

8. Not quick to understand

Down

1. Regional form of a language

2. Energetic state

7. The process of obtaining or procuring something

9. Boundary of an object or area

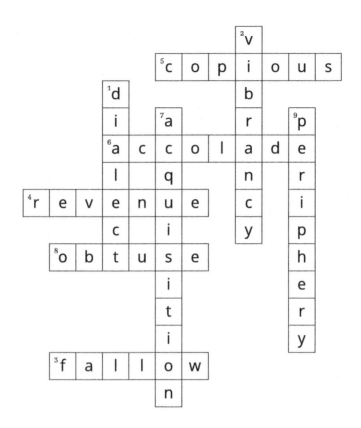

Across

3. Land left to restore fertility

4. Income from business operations

5. Plentiful

6. Privilege granted as an honor

8. Not quick to understand

Down

1. Regional form of a language

2. Energetic state

7. The process of obtaining or procuring something

9. Boundary of an object or area

Across

1. Smallest speck
4. Familiarity in a new situation
5. Less is more advocate
6. Clumsy operation
7. Related to a powerful creative individual

Down

2. Unquestionably true
3. Principle for judgment
8. Those engaged in an organized activity
9. Lavish generosity
10. Planned enterprise to achieve a goal

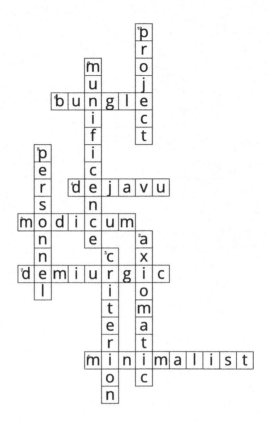

Across

1. Smallest speck

4. Familiarity in a new situation

5. Less is more advocate

6. Clumsy operation

7. Related to a powerful creative individual

Down

2. Unquestionably true

3. Principle for judgment

8. Those engaged in an organized activity

9. Lavish generosity

10. Planned enterprise to achieve a goal

Across

2. Simultaneous tasks handler

3. Made very happy

6. The conclusion indicator

9. Highest person in a corporation

10. Expression of grief or concern

Down

1. Intentionally misleading clue

4. Full of friendliness

5. Extremely harmful in effect

7. Extreme amusement

8. Informal or familiar speech

Across

2. Simultaneous tasks handler

3. Made very happy

6. The conclusion indicator

9. Highest person in a corporation

10. Expression of grief or concern

Down

1. Intentionally misleading clue

4. Full of friendliness

5. Extremely harmful in effect

7. Extreme amusement

8. Informal or familiar speech

Across

1. The act of reading closely

4. Improvement action

5. Overused to the point of staleness

6. Have an intense feeling of missing something

7. Tolerant of pain

Down

2. Eager to achieve

3. A company's financial statement

8. Poetic device for comparison

9. Self-admirer to a fault

10. Unique to a subject

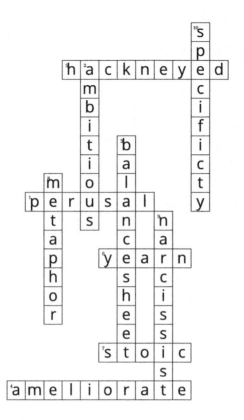

Across

1. The act of reading closely
4. Improvement action
5. Overused to the point of staleness
6. Have an intense feeling of missing something
7. Tolerant of pain

Down

2. Eager to achieve
3. A company's financial statement
8. Poetic device for comparison
9. Self-admirer to a fault
10. Unique to a subject

Across

1. Lacking transparency

3. Can't see through it

5. Flagrantly bad

7. Date for task completion

9. Increasing progressively

Down

2. Words that sound alike but differ in meaning

4. Loud and insistent

6. Rudely intrusive

8. Cunning and deceptive

10. Displaying great knowledge

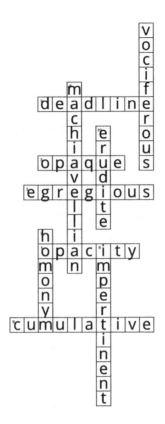

Across

1. Lacking transparency

3. Can't see through it

5. Flagrantly bad

7. Date for task completion

9. Increasing progressively

Down

2. Words that sound alike but differ in meaning

4. Loud and insistent

6. Rudely intrusive

8. Cunning and deceptive

10. Displaying great knowledge

Across

1. Outstandingly bad

3. Skeptical of human integrity

5. Capable of success

9. Work of keeping financial accounts

10. Lack of seriousness

Down

2. Coming together into one

4. Reciprocal agreement

6. Lengthy criticism or accusation

7. Perfect representation of a class

8. Gained through deception

Crossword

Across
1. Outstandingly bad
3. Skeptical of human integrity
5. Capable of success
9. Work of keeping financial accounts
10. Lack of seriousness

Down
2. Coming together into one
4. Reciprocal agreement
6. Lengthy criticism or accusation
7. Perfect representation of a class
8. Gained through deception

Across

4. A source of stability

5. Major action plan

7. Firmly adhering

8. Extreme laughter or amusement

9. Time limit

Down

1. Overscrupulousness

2. Disrespectfully bold

3. Deceptively damaging

6. Servile flatterer

10. Contemplative consideration

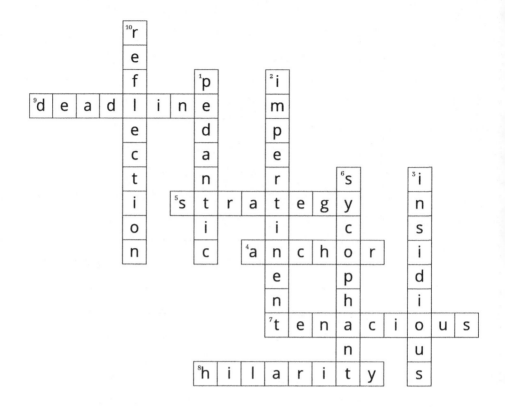

Across

4. A source of stability

5. Major action plan

7. Firmly adhering

8. Extreme laughter or amusement

9. Time limit

Down

1. Overscrupulousness

2. Disrespectfully bold

3. Deceptively damaging

6. Servile flatterer

10. Contemplative consideration

Across

2. Genuinely real

3. Spend foolishly

4. Coming into view

7. Desire deeply for something lost or separated from

8. Complete failure

Down

1. Averse to effort

5. Detail-obsessed teaching

6. Tousled or unkempt

9. It's like this

10. Inspiring charm

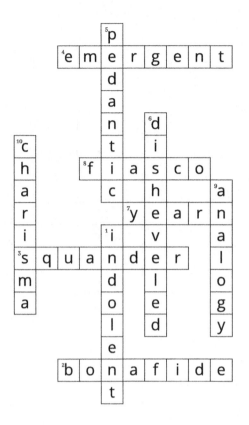

Across

2. Genuinely real

3. Spend foolishly

4. Coming into view

7. Desire deeply for something lost or separated from

8. Complete failure

Down

1. Averse to effort

5. Detail-obsessed teaching

6. Tousled or unkempt

9. It's like this

10. Inspiring charm

Across

2. Single speaker in a play
3. Inappropriate stare
4. Creditor's claim
8. Criticize sharply
10. Sedate or sober

Down

1. Ease an action or process
5. Lazily inactive
6. Technical or niche language
7. Contrary to religious orthodoxy
9. Ethics for sale?

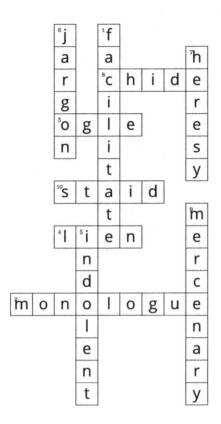

Across

2. Single speaker in a play

3. Inappropriate stare

4. Creditor's claim

8. Criticize sharply

10. Sedate or sober

Down

1. Ease an action or process

5. Lazily inactive

6. Technical or niche language

7. Contrary to religious orthodoxy

9. Ethics for sale?

Across

1. Additionally considering

2. Overcome with despair

3. Implementation of complex tasks

5. Avoid work by faking sickness

9. Rapidly increasing

Down

4. Paid warrior without loyalty

6. Non-drinker by principle

7. Detailed planning and coordination

8. Fearlessly determined

10. Extremely minute

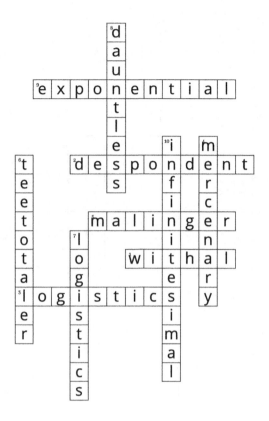

Across

1. Additionally considering
2. Overcome with despair
3. Implementation of complex tasks
5. Avoid work by faking sickness
9. Rapidly increasing

Down

4. Paid warrior without loyalty
6. Non-drinker by principle
7. Detailed planning and coordination
8. Fearlessly determined
10. Extremely minute

Across

2. Insufficiency of something

3. Stage for performers

5. Badge of dishonor

7. Attribution to source materials

9. Frequently stated phrase

Down

1. Long-standing adversary

4. Trust among frequent companions

6. Overly sentimental art

8. Evolution of static web to dynamic social media

10. Achieved with speed and efficiency

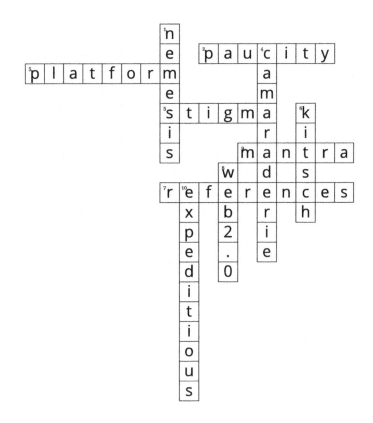

Across

2. Insufficiency of something
3. Stage for performers
5. Badge of dishonor
7. Attribution to source materials
9. Frequently stated phrase

Down

1. Long-standing adversary
4. Trust among frequent companions
6. Overly sentimental art
8. Evolution of static web to dynamic social media
10. Achieved with speed and efficiency

Across

1. Biblically ancient
4. Product identity promotion
5. Corrosively sarcastic
9. Lowest ebb
10. A description of an experience

Down

2. Comprehension via intellect
3. Reluctance to spend
6. Epitome of a quality
7. Individual oddity
8. Team up for an activity

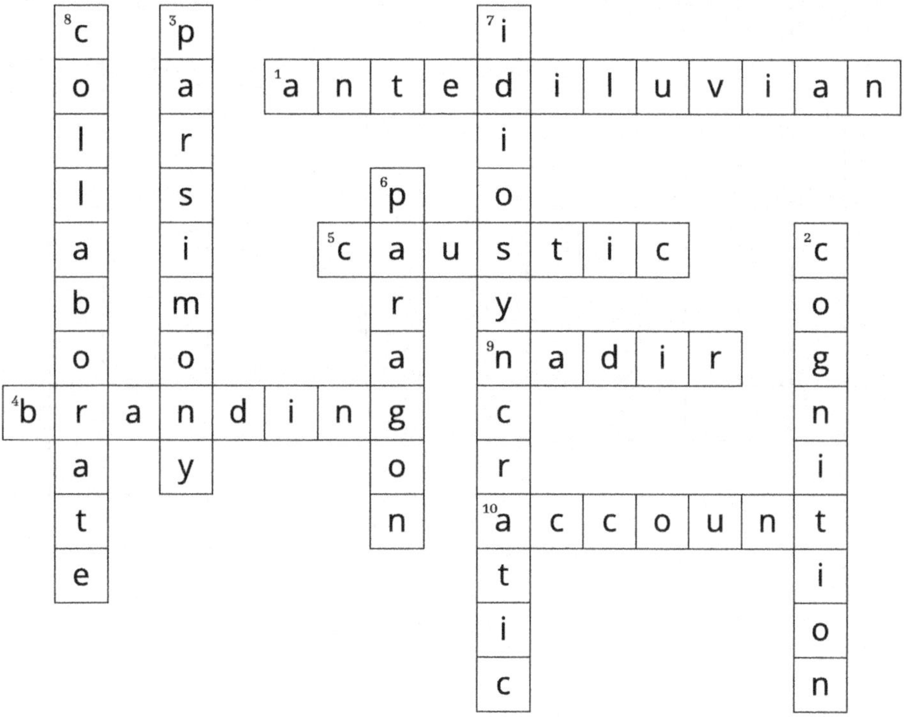
antediluvian
branding
caustic
nadir
account
cognition
parsimony
paragon
idiosyncratic
collaborate

Across

1. Biblically ancient
4. Product identity promotion
5. Corrosively sarcastic
9. Lowest ebb
10. A description of an experience

Down

2. Comprehension via intellect
3. Reluctance to spend
6. Epitome of a quality
7. Individual oddity
8. Team up for an activity

Across

2. Bubble up from a liquid

3. Gradually ineffective

4. Acquire dishonestly

6. Brazenly disrespectful

7. Rebuke

Down

1. Group gathering

5. Connection between two variables

8. Expressive and moving

9. Most conspicuous

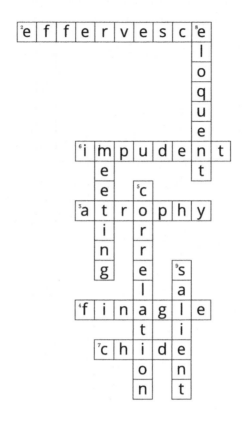

Across

2. Bubble up from a liquid

3. Gradually ineffective

4. Acquire dishonestly

6. Brazenly disrespectful

7. Rebuke

Down

1. Group gathering

5. Connection between two variables

8. Expressive and moving

9. Most conspicuous

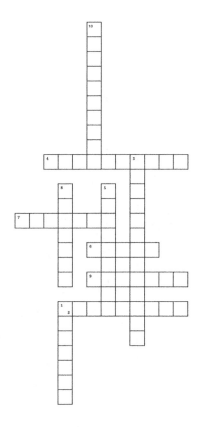

Across

2. Harmony in opinion or feeling

4. Melodious or pleasant-sounding

6. Celebration with guests

7. Paramount in stature

9. Hastily and superficially performed

Down

1. Abbreviation pronounced as a word

3. Unbelievably tiny

5. Occurring too soon

8. Dishonest for personal gain

10. From this point onward

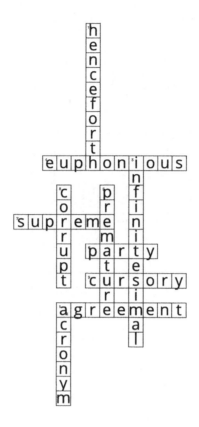

Across

2. Harmony in opinion or feeling

4. Melodious or pleasant-sounding

6. Celebration with guests

7. Paramount in stature

9. Hastily and superficially performed

Down

1. Abbreviation pronounced as a word

3. Unbelievably tiny

5. Occurring too soon

8. Dishonest for personal gain

10. From this point onward

Across

1. Getting services from outside
2. Period equivalent to 1/4th of a year
4. Disclose confidential information
8. Publicly express strong disapproval
9. Reckless in spending

Down

3. Kind and compassionate
5. Speech or talk to show and explain something
6. Section for pushing products or services
7. Report or narration of an event
10. Legal pact

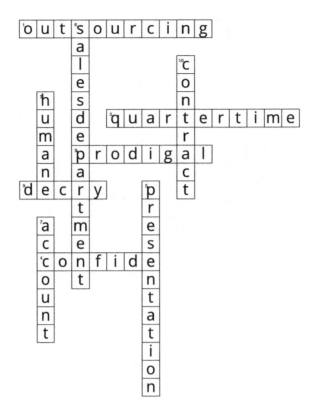

Across

1. Getting services from outside
2. Period equivalent to 1/4th of a year
4. Disclose confidential information
8. Publicly express strong disapproval
9. Reckless in spending

Down

3. Kind and compassionate
5. Speech or talk to show and explain something
6. Section for pushing products or services
7. Report or narration of an event
10. Legal pact

Across

1. Pacify someone's anger
4. Incompatible with surroundings
7. Intensely damaging or destructive
8. Offhand manner
9. Smug satisfaction

Down

2. Spending of funds
3. Placate to calm
5. Conceding to opponent's demand
6. Hard to understand or know
10. When underuse leads to decline

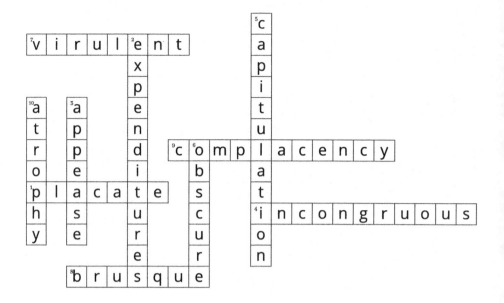

Across
1. Pacify someone's anger
4. Incompatible with surroundings
7. Intensely damaging or destructive
8. Offhand manner
9. Smug satisfaction

Down
2. Spending of funds
3. Placate to calm
5. Conceding to opponent's demand
6. Hard to understand or know
10. When underuse leads to decline

Across

1. Significant swerve from the usual

3. Efficient and speedy

5. Unappeasably resolute

6. Define without ambiguity

10. Burst open abruptly

Down

2. Pertaining to the nature of being

4. State of being unknown

7. Grandeur in architecture

8. Regular tendency to choose something

9. Art of teaching

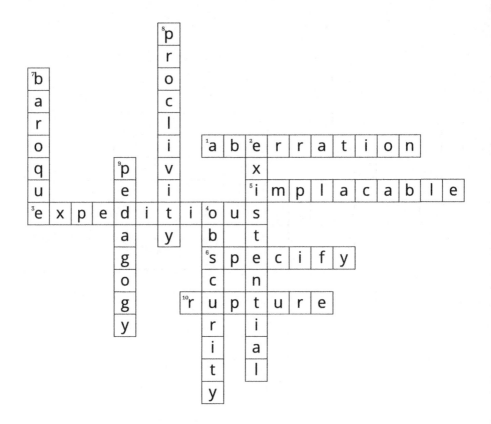

Across

1. Significant swerve from the usual

3. Efficient and speedy

5. Unappeasably resolute

6. Define without ambiguity

10. Burst open abruptly

Down

2. Pertaining to the nature of being

4. State of being unknown

7. Grandeur in architecture

8. Regular tendency to choose something

9. Art of teaching

Across

1. Annoyance or displeasure

2. Unite in a common end

4. Critical humor

6. Pollute a substance

8. Perfectly peaceful

Down

3. Making money from something

5. Thoughts spoken aloud

7. Withdraw a law or agreement

9. Restrict or deter

10. Voluntarily leave a position

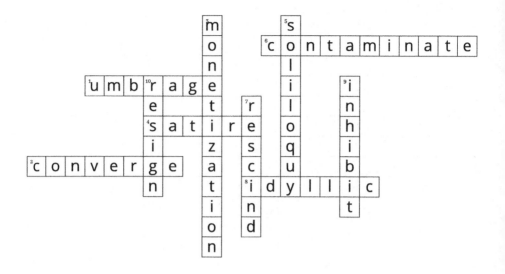

Across

1. Annoyance or displeasure

2. Unite in a common end

4. Critical humor

6. Pollute a substance

8. Perfectly peaceful

Down

3. Making money from something

5. Thoughts spoken aloud

7. Withdraw a law or agreement

9. Restrict or deter

10. Voluntarily leave a position

Across

2. Difference between facts

3. Word choice in speech or writing

4. Extraction from a danger zone

6. Inexperienced individual

7. Shout at length in anger

Down

1. Move someone to safety

5. Unquestionably certain

8. A strong liking

9. Obtain by devious means

10. Improper

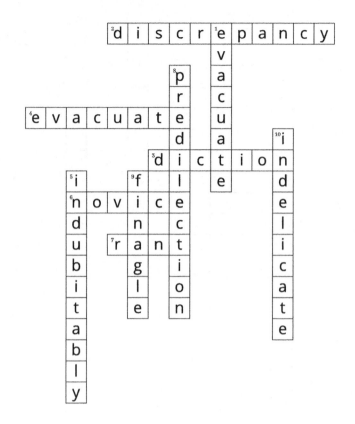

Across

2. Difference between facts

3. Word choice in speech or writing

4. Extraction from a danger zone

6. Inexperienced individual

7. Shout at length in anger

Down

1. Move someone to safety

5. Unquestionably certain

8. A strong liking

9. Obtain by devious means

10. Improper

Across

1. Not just strange

4. Knowledgeable through study

7. The edge of something

8. Pretend to be sick

9. Absolute bottom

Down

2. Poison counteract

3. Wary of danger

5. Growing at an increasing rate

6. To disavow or reject

10. Funny in an unconventional way

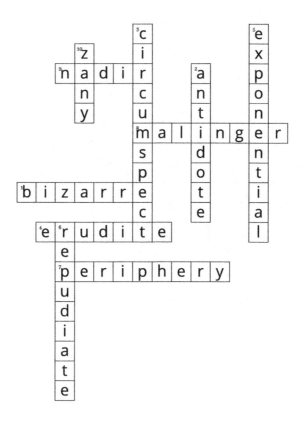

Across

1. Not just strange
4. Knowledgeable through study
7. The edge of something
8. Pretend to be sick
9. Absolute bottom

Down

2. Poison counteract
3. Wary of danger
5. Growing at an increasing rate
6. To disavow or reject
10. Funny in an unconventional way

Across

3. Not showing suffering

4. Wealth's insatiable pursuit

5. Denounce or condemn openly

6. Specialized speak

7. Same-sounding words with different meanings

Down

1. Revered for wisdom or character

2. Process of merging

8. Scarcity or lack

9. Fixed compensation

10. Generally or widely accepted

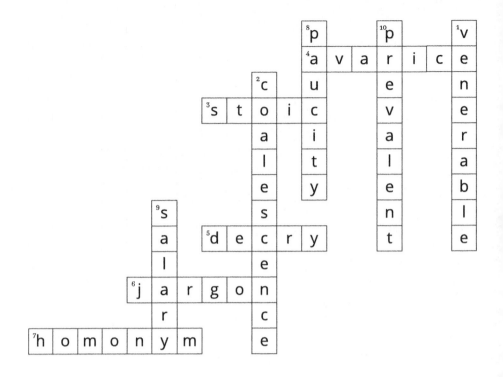

Across

3. Not showing suffering
4. Wealth's insatiable pursuit
5. Denounce or condemn openly
6. Specialized speak
7. Same-sounding words with different meanings

Down

1. Revered for wisdom or character
2. Process of merging
8. Scarcity or lack
9. Fixed compensation
10. Generally or widely accepted

Across

1. Amicable relations

5. More than just cordial

7. Deviating

9. Second phase of internet development

10. Laugh out loud

Down

2. Digital data management

3. Secret meeting

4. Startup financing

6. Shamelessly bold

8. One abstaining from alcohol

Across

1. Amicable relations

5. More than just cordial

7. Deviating

9. Second phase of internet development

10. Laugh out loud

Down

2. Digital data management

3. Secret meeting

4. Startup financing

6. Shamelessly bold

8. One abstaining from alcohol

Across

1. Amplify

2. Only titular

5. Driven by success

6. Regular trading gathering

7. General expectations

Down

3. Alias especially for writers

4. Disastrous event

8. Tacitly encourage harm

9. Extended rant

10. Over-the-top praise or admiration

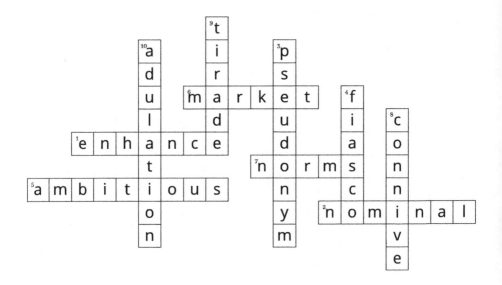

Across

1. Amplify
2. Only titular
5. Driven by success
6. Regular trading gathering
7. General expectations

Down

3. Alias especially for writers
4. Disastrous event
8. Tacitly encourage harm
9. Extended rant
10. Over-the-top praise or admiration

Across

1. State of non-translucence

2. Flexibly graceful

4. An error due to stupidity

6. Sentence structure

7. Mild substitute for a harsh term

Down

3. Remove from danger to a safe place

5. State of being stretched out

8. Extremely attentive to detail

9. Overseer of operations

10. Set in motion

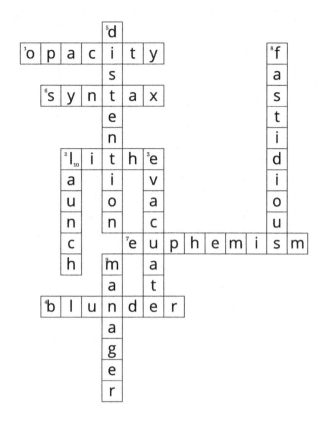

Across

1. State of non-translucence
2. Flexibly graceful
4. An error due to stupidity
6. Sentence structure
7. Mild substitute for a harsh term

Down

3. Remove from danger to a safe place
5. State of being stretched out
8. Extremely attentive to detail
9. Overseer of operations
10. Set in motion

Across

2. Deep-rooted habit
3. Impermanent status
4. Instructive with a moral aim
5. Phrases for concepts
10. Disgust and hatred combined

Down

1. Update and restore to good condition
6. Can be used up and replaced
7. Unorthodox belief or opinion
8. Work towards improving products and processes
9. Insensitive disregard

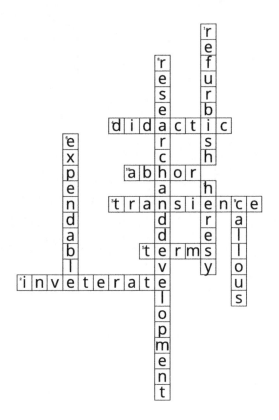

Across

2. Deep-rooted habit

3. Impermanent status

4. Instructive with a moral aim

5. Phrases for concepts

10. Disgust and hatred combined

Down

1. Update and restore to good condition

6. Can be used up and replaced

7. Unorthodox belief or opinion

8. Work towards improving products and processes

9. Insensitive disregard

Across

3. Willing to take risks
4. Studying something with attention
5. Collective accord
6. Topmost in rank
7. Free of cost or unearned

Down

1. Profit-driven founder
2. Recurring business expenditure
8. Process of control
9. Exclusion from group
10. Contrasting placement

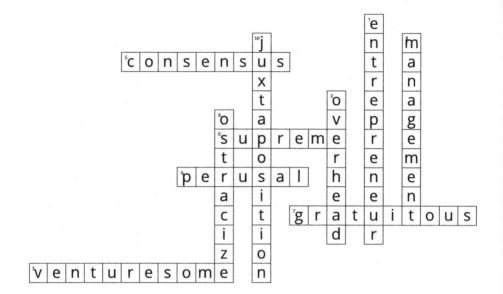

Across

3. Willing to take risks

4. Studying something with attention

5. Collective accord

6. Topmost in rank

7. Free of cost or unearned

Down

1. Profit-driven founder

2. Recurring business expenditure

8. Process of control

9. Exclusion from group

10. Contrasting placement

Across

3. Satirical imitation

4. Short-lived state

6. Pithy saying

9. Discordant sound mixture

10. Vehemently noisy or outspoken

Down

1. Something difficult to understand

2. To back up with evidence

5. End user of services

7. Unthinkable

8. Uninterested in other cultures

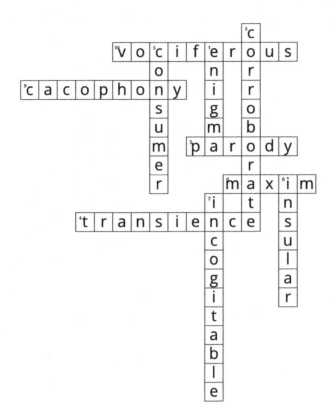

Across

3. Satirical imitation

4. Short-lived state

6. Pithy saying

9. Discordant sound mixture

10. Vehemently noisy or outspoken

Down

1. Something difficult to understand

2. To back up with evidence

5. End user of services

7. Unthinkable

8. Uninterested in other cultures

Across

4. Luxurious and expensive-looking

5. Recurring theme in art

8. Intelligently clear-thinking

9. A great source of vexation

10. Sophisticated charm

Down

1. Secretively

2. Workforce of an organization

3. Beginner in a job

6. Sentimentality in excess

7. Long intensely for something

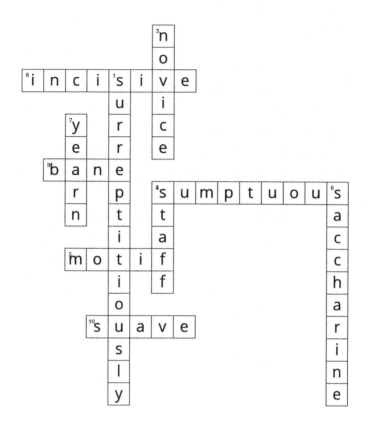

Across

4. Luxurious and expensive-looking

5. Recurring theme in art

8. Intelligently clear-thinking

9. A great source of vexation

10. Sophisticated charm

Down

1. Secretively

2. Workforce of an organization

3. Beginner in a job

6. Sentimentality in excess

7. Long intensely for something

Across

2. Reserved in manner

4. Unsown but prepared land

7. Chief Executive Officer

8. Overly emotional

9. Non-variable operation expenses

Down

1. Merge together

3. Secretive

5. Tirelessly attentive

6. Abundant to an extreme

10. Clearly defined or determined

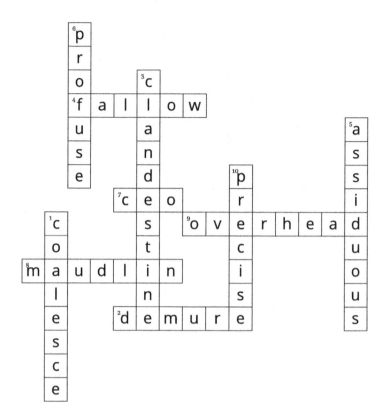

Across

2. Reserved in manner

4. Unsown but prepared land

7. Chief Executive Officer

8. Overly emotional

9. Non-variable operation expenses

Down

1. Merge together

3. Secretive

5. Tirelessly attentive

6. Abundant to an extreme

10. Clearly defined or determined

Across

1. Characteristic of being exact and accurate
3. Of a creative force
5. Identify clearly
6. Quick to irritate
7. Predisposition for a preference

Down

2. Buyer for personal use
4. Money placement for return
8. Kept secret
9. Compassion in judgement
10. Tend to one result or conclusion

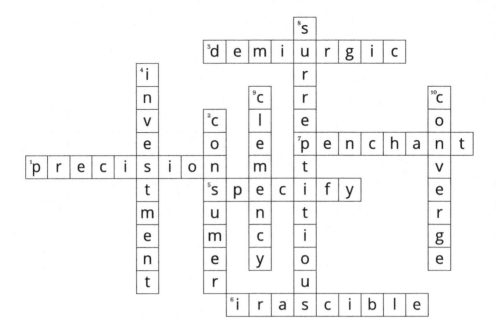

Across

1. Characteristic of being exact and accurate

3. Of a creative force

5. Identify clearly

6. Quick to irritate

7. Predisposition for a preference

Down

2. Buyer for personal use

4. Money placement for return

8. Kept secret

9. Compassion in judgement

10. Tend to one result or conclusion

Across

2. Productive or constructive

3. Contrary meaning

5. Showing intense enthusiasm or passion

8. Non-conformist individual

10. Pertaining to Byzantium

Down

1. Retain for future use

4. Study of sound systems in languages

6. Buzz or hiss

7. Assets and liabilities snapshot

9. Tedium

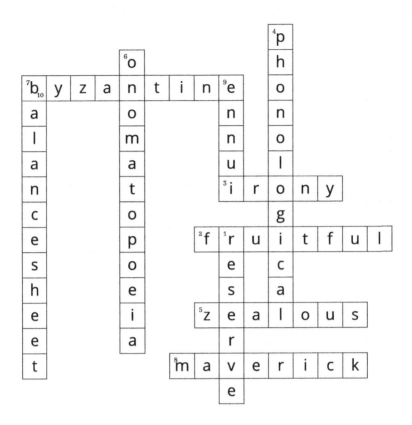

Across

2. Productive or constructive

3. Contrary meaning

5. Showing intense enthusiasm or passion

8. Non-conformist individual

10. Pertaining to Byzantium

Down

1. Retain for future use

4. Study of sound systems in languages

6. Buzz or hiss

7. Assets and liabilities snapshot

9. Tedium

Across

2. Shockingly vivid

3. Cannot be defended

6. Disdainfully proud

7. Boldly fearless

8. Float easily as if on air

Down

1. Exquisite and faultless

4. Commercial activity branch

5. Economic organization

9. Put a spanner in the works

10. Unjustly virtuous

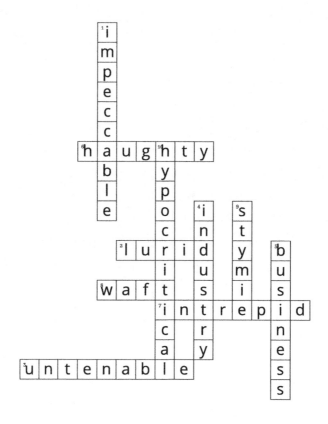

Across

2. Shockingly vivid
3. Cannot be defended
6. Disdainfully proud
7. Boldly fearless
8. Float easily as if on air

Down

1. Exquisite and faultless
4. Commercial activity branch
5. Economic organization
9. Put a spanner in the works
10. Unjustly virtuous

Across

1. Smoothly confident
2. Inordinate admiration or praise
4. Obsequious person
5. Financial buffer
6. Word or phrase for describing

Down

3. Resistant to authority
7. Characteristically sulky
8. Legal monetary debt
9. Ill feeling or animosity
10. Bumbling oaf

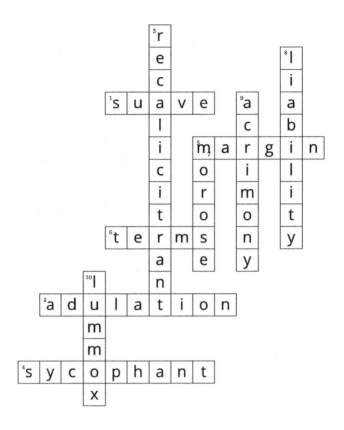

Across

1. Smoothly confident

2. Inordinate admiration or praise

4. Obsequious person

5. Financial buffer

6. Word or phrase for describing

Down

3. Resistant to authority

7. Characteristically sulky

8. Legal monetary debt

9. Ill feeling or animosity

10. Bumbling oaf

Across

2. Herald of upcoming events

6. Subtle difference

7. Control of something harmful

9. Cancel or retract a decision

10. Endurer of hardship

Down

1. Universal cure-all

3. Financial supporter of activity

4. Mental process of knowledge acquisition

5. Yielding to judgment

8. Unrestricted authority

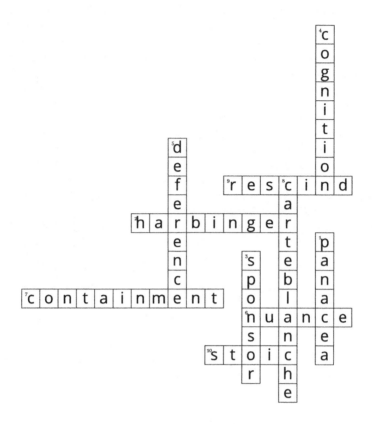

Across

2. Herald of upcoming events

6. Subtle difference

7. Control of something harmful

9. Cancel or retract a decision

10. Endurer of hardship

Down

1. Universal cure-all

3. Financial supporter of activity

4. Mental process of knowledge acquisition

5. Yielding to judgment

8. Unrestricted authority

Across

3. Process of maintaining financial records
4. Nearly identical in severity
7. Reject disdainfully
8. Clarified rewording
9. Clumsy fool

Down

1. Entity for monetary transactions
2. Bungling
5. Working remotely via internet
6. Inherently wicked
10. Universally present

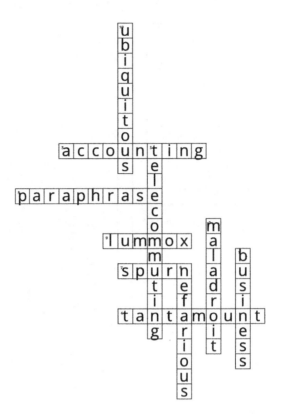

Across

3. Process of maintaining financial records
4. Nearly identical in severity
7. Reject disdainfully
8. Clarified rewording
9. Clumsy fool

Down

1. Entity for monetary transactions
2. Bungling
5. Working remotely via internet
6. Inherently wicked
10. Universally present

Across

1. Promoting health

3. Well-supplied with something

4. A fiscal forecast

9. Down in the dumps

10. A negative aspect

Down

2. Conscientious in duties

5. Cautious

6. Repeating vowels in poetry

7. Filled with pride

8. Busywork with no value

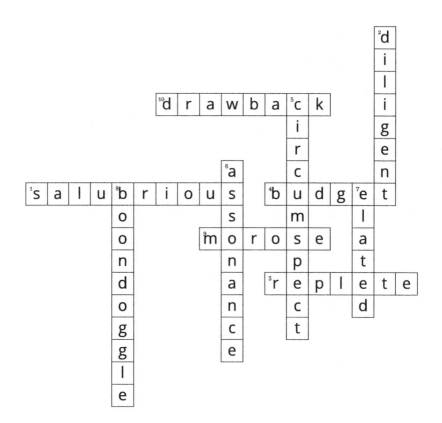

Across

1. Promoting health

3. Well-supplied with something

4. A fiscal forecast

9. Down in the dumps

10. A negative aspect

Down

2. Conscientious in duties

5. Cautious

6. Repeating vowels in poetry

7. Filled with pride

8. Busywork with no value

Across

2. Clamorously expressing opinions
3. Cooperatively work together
5. Act of defaming
9. Mystery
10. Shrinking an organization by cutting jobs

Down

1. Profit for purpose
4. Non-specific feeling of illness
6. Happy chance
7. Hold something dear
8. Harshness of tone or manner

Across

2. Clamorously expressing opinions
3. Cooperatively work together
5. Act of defaming
9. Mystery
10. Shrinking an organization by cutting jobs

Down

1. Profit for purpose
4. Non-specific feeling of illness
6. Happy chance
7. Hold something dear
8. Harshness of tone or manner

Across

4. Above ordinary range

5. Shorten text while keeping essence

6. Concise explanation

8. Overstatement for effect

10. Administrator or supervisor

Down

1. Low in spirits

2. Leave completely and finally

3. Exhibiting beauty

7. Unethical conduct by authorities

9. Remedy for all ills

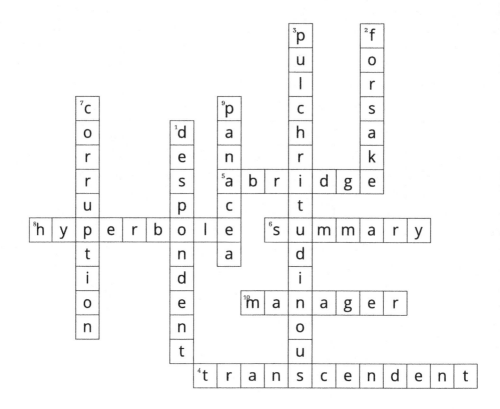

Across

4. Above ordinary range
5. Shorten text while keeping essence
6. Concise explanation
8. Overstatement for effect
10. Administrator or supervisor

Down

1. Low in spirits
2. Leave completely and finally
3. Exhibiting beauty
7. Unethical conduct by authorities
9. Remedy for all ills

Across

1. Overjoyed

2. Simplify a process

5. Reluctantly accept without protest

9. Use of words in language

10. Purposeful assembly

Down

3. Relating to development

4. Emit small bubbles

6. Construct or manufacture

7. Careless mistake

8. Sought out with care

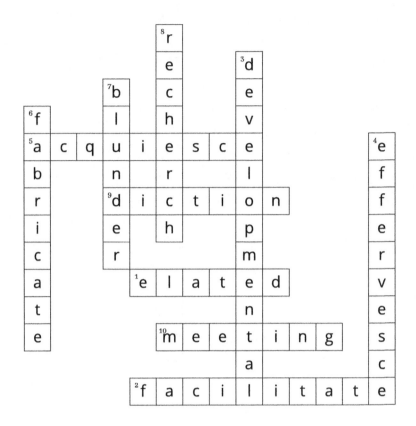

Across

1. Overjoyed

2. Simplify a process

5. Reluctantly accept without protest

9. Use of words in language

10. Purposeful assembly

Down

3. Relating to development

4. Emit small bubbles

6. Construct or manufacture

7. Careless mistake

8. Sought out with care

Across

1. Surprise or confuse

3. Full of a particular attribute

6. Hard to understand

7. Child of the streets

9. Smooth but shallow

Down

2. Flavorful and appetizing

4. Thing already decided or happened

5. Abhor or despise

8. Secret sharer

10. Approve provision of

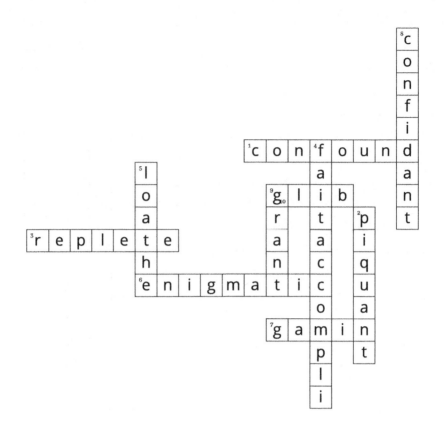

Across

1. Surprise or confuse

3. Full of a particular attribute

6. Hard to understand

7. Child of the streets

9. Smooth but shallow

Down

2. Flavorful and appetizing

4. Thing already decided or happened

5. Abhor or despise

8. Secret sharer

10. Approve provision of

Across

2. Coagulate

4. Occurring after one's demise

6. Ruler with absolute power

7. Impulsive action without thought

8. Without a plan

Down

1. Mildness in punishment

3. Contracting work out

5. Person-to-person marketing strategy

9. Commonly spoken language

10. Exuberantly plentiful

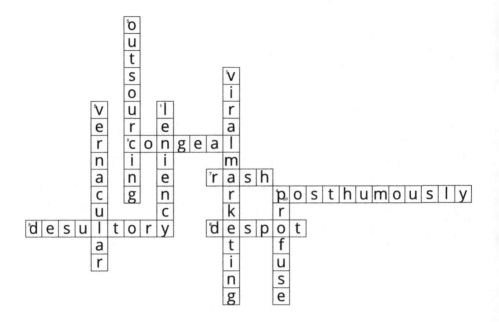

Across

2. Coagulate

4. Occurring after one's demise

6. Ruler with absolute power

7. Impulsive action without thought

8. Without a plan

Down

1. Mildness in punishment

3. Contracting work out

5. Person-to-person marketing strategy

9. Commonly spoken language

10. Exuberantly plentiful

Across

1. Arch rival
2. Full of energy
5. Idea invoked by a word
9. Difference between income and expenditure
10. Boredom

Down

3. Group problem-solving technique
4. Too sweet to stomach
6. Main office or central department
7. To collect or gather
8. Ceasing to resist

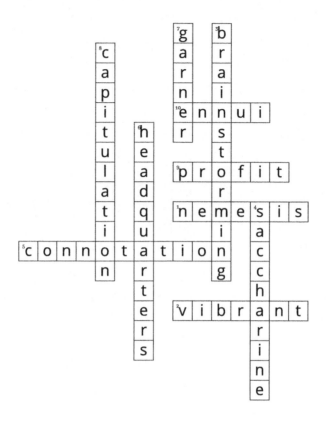

Across

1. Arch rival
2. Full of energy
5. Idea invoked by a word
9. Difference between income and expenditure
10. Boredom

Down

3. Group problem-solving technique
4. Too sweet to stomach
6. Main office or central department
7. To collect or gather
8. Ceasing to resist

Across

2. Exchange of contacts
6. Tending to be different
7. Initial letters forming a pronounceable abbreviation
8. Comical imitation
9. Give up a role or position

Down

1. Inconsistent in behavior
3. Artful expressiveness
4. Tedious recount
5. Deny access to a place
10. Tiny portion

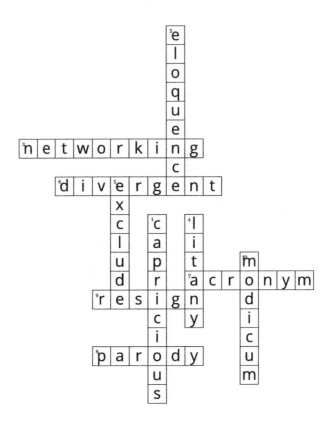

Across

2. Exchange of contacts

6. Tending to be different

7. Initial letters forming a pronounceable abbreviation

8. Comical imitation

9. Give up a role or position

Down

1. Inconsistent in behavior

3. Artful expressiveness

4. Tedious recount

5. Deny access to a place

10. Tiny portion

Across

1. Disturbance in air or water

2. Unanimous decision

3. To remedy a situation

4. Disturb smoothness of hair

5. An argument

8. Artistic dominant idea

Down

6. Lack of compatibility

7. Stamp of a company on its product

9. Break suddenly

10. Hover in air

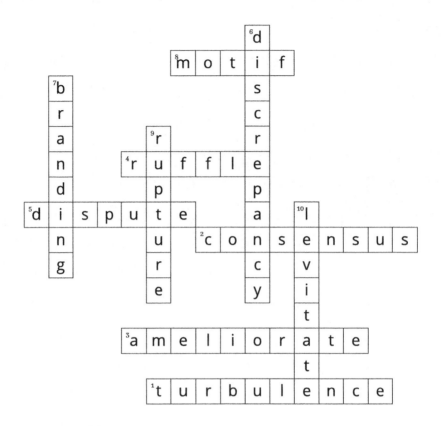

Across

1. Disturbance in air or water

2. Unanimous decision

3. To remedy a situation

4. Disturb smoothness of hair

5. An argument

8. Artistic dominant idea

Down

6. Lack of compatibility

7. Stamp of a company on its product

9. Break suddenly

10. Hover in air

Across

1. Declines from neglect

5. Premise for proving

7. Unjustifiable position

8. Respected due to age

9. Usable and discardable

Down

2. Sweet curd dish

3. Beyond imagination

4. Ineffective

6. Enjoying gatherings

10. Financial obligation

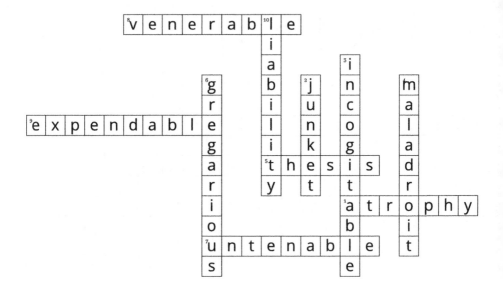

Across

1. Declines from neglect

5. Premise for proving

7. Unjustifiable position

8. Respected due to age

9. Usable and discardable

Down

2. Sweet curd dish

3. Beyond imagination

4. Ineffective

6. Enjoying gatherings

10. Financial obligation

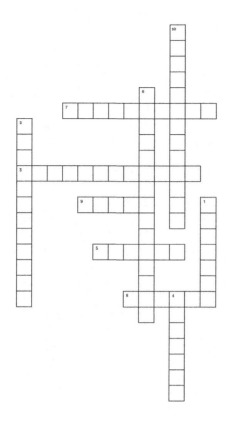

Across

3. Conversion rate for currencies

5. Hostility

7. Unctuously compliant

8. Attractively old-fashioned

9. Very proficient at something

Down

1. Outstandingly noticeable

2. Turning assets into legal tender

4. Driving force

6. Visually appealing

10. Working away from office via technology

Across

3. Conversion rate for currencies

5. Hostility

7. Unctuously compliant

8. Attractively old-fashioned

9. Very proficient at something

Down

1. Outstandingly noticeable

2. Turning assets into legal tender

4. Driving force

6. Visually appealing

10. Working away from office via technology

Across

3. It's useful or beneficial

5. Comparative rhetoric

6. Remarkably large in degree

8. Renovate and redecorate

10. Speaking with multiple interpretations

Down

1. A disagreement or difference of opinion

2. Crush or grind into dust

4. Reducing the number of employees

7. On top in influence

9. Lacking understanding of the arts

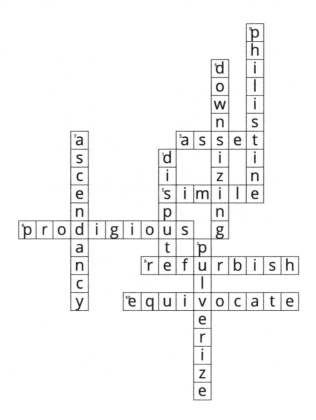

Across

3. It's useful or beneficial
5. Comparative rhetoric
6. Remarkably large in degree
8. Renovate and redecorate
10. Speaking with multiple interpretations

Down

1. A disagreement or difference of opinion
2. Crush or grind into dust
4. Reducing the number of employees
7. On top in influence
9. Lacking understanding of the arts

Across

1. Risk averse
2. Quick to argue
6. Tearfully sentimental
8. Drift slowly and lightly
10. European architectural style

Down

3. Lacking in purpose
4. Intentionally confuse
5. Planned in advance
7. It's unclear which way this goes
9. Not harmonizing

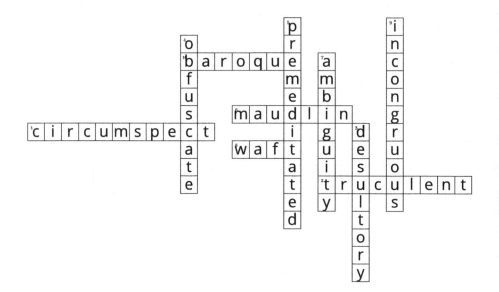

Across

1. Risk averse

2. Quick to argue

6. Tearfully sentimental

8. Drift slowly and lightly

10. European architectural style

Down

3. Lacking in purpose

4. Intentionally confuse

5. Planned in advance

7. It's unclear which way this goes

9. Not harmonizing

Across

4. Feeling of previous experience

8. Tainted with dishonesty

9. Insignificance or anonymity

10. Repulsive to look at

Down

1. Develop in a healthy way

2. Abundant in quantity

3. Action of advancing in rank

5. Amateur in a field of knowledge

7. Splendid and opulent

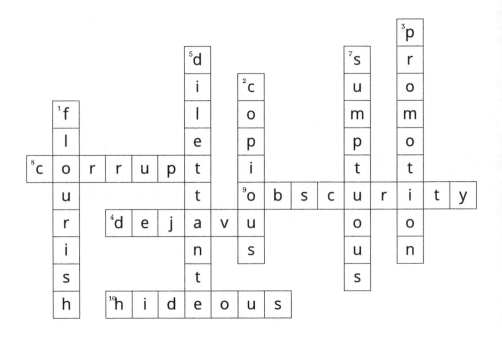

Across

4. Feeling of previous experience

8. Tainted with dishonesty

9. Insignificance or anonymity

10. Repulsive to look at

Down

1. Develop in a healthy way

2. Abundant in quantity

3. Action of advancing in rank

5. Amateur in a field of knowledge

7. Splendid and opulent

my words to watch

my words to watch

my words to watch

Free Puzzles

Get 200 free math and word games.

Made in the USA
Monee, IL
01 October 2023

43787827R00063